THE ASTROLOGER'S SPARROW

For Dear Martina

w/ Best wishes

From Panova

September 21, 2022

Washington DC

"My life is in your hands!"

Also by New Academia Publishing

ONYX MOON: Poems, by J. H. Beall
Winner of the 2018 William Meredith Foundation Award for Poetry.

INSIDE OUTSIDE: Poems, by Sue Silver

NO BARKING IN THE HALLWAYS: Poems for the Classroom, by Ann Bracken

AT THE END OF THE SELF-HELP ROPE: Poems, by Ed Zahniser

MASS FOR NANKING'S 1937, by Wing-chi Chan

THE HOUR OF THE POEM POEM: Poems on Writing, by David Bristol

THE WHITE SPIDER IN MY HAND: Poems, by Sonja James

THE ALTAR OF INNOCENCE: Poems, by Ann Bracken

THE MAN WHO GOT AWAY: Poems, by Grace Cavalieri

IN BLACK BEAR COUNTRY, by Maureen Waters

ALWAYS THE TRAINS: Poems, by Judy Neri

Read an excerpt at www.newacademia.com

THE ASTROLOGER'S SPARROW

POEMS BY

Panna Naik

NEW ACADEMIA PUBLISHING | SCARITH

WASHINGTON, DC

THE ASTROLOGER'S SPARROW
Copyright © 2018 by Panna Naik

New Academia Publishing 2018

Cover design by Janice Olson. (Image CC0.)

Printed in the United States of America

Library of Congress Control Number: 2018957867
ISBN: 978-1-7326988-1-9 paperback (alk. paper)

 An imprint of New Academia Publishing

 New Academia Publishing
4401-A Connecticut Avenue NW #236
Washington DC 20008
info@newacademia.com
www.newacademia.com

For Suresh Dalal, who is no more.

CONTENTS

CONTENTS

ACKNOWLEDGEMENTS

I have been writing poetry in Gujarati, a major Indian language, for nearly 40 years. During that time, the late Suresh Dalal, an eminent Gujarati poet, dear friend and mentor took a special interest in my writing and I am deeply grateful.

Numerous friends and colleagues have also provided support as writing in English was a new venture for me. I am particularly grateful to:

The late P. Sreenivasa Rao, Saleem Peeradina, Mira Desai and Eleanor Wilner.

Roshni Rustomji-Kerns, Carlo Coppola and Pradyumna Chauhan have taken an interest in my poetry ever since I began writing four decades ago, and generously provided commentary.

Pamela Sutton, a distinguished poet herself, whose collaboration has been invaluable. Her critical comments substantially improved the manuscript and contributed to the shape of the work.

Grace Cavalieri, ever gracious and noted poet for her continuous encouragement and my publisher, Anna Lawton, for her enthusiastic support.

Special thanks to the book designer, Janice Olson, and to Jenna Lordo for providing administrative support.

Above all, I thank Natwar Gandhi, my life partner and companion who has been with me in my life's journey with abundant love and care.

What would happen if one woman told the
truth about her life?
The world would split open.

— Muriel Rukeyser, "Kathe Kollwitz"
from *The Speed of Darkness*

She died of internal weeping.
— Eleanor Ross Taylor

But I make no excuses
I believe that seeking beautiful words is better
than killing murdering.
— Jaroslav Seifert

You may write me down in history
With your bitter, twisted lies,
You may trod me in the very dirt
But still, like dust, I'll rise.
— Maya Angelou

Arranging Birds

In front of me,
a paper like a piece of sky
cut up just right;
and with it,
I play the game
of arranging birds.

Is it ever possible
to control a bird in the sky?
A bird cannot perch
in a sky without branches.
Even after soaring in the clouds
and returning exhausted to the Earth,
the bird yearns for sky.
Who owns the sky?
The Sun or the Moon?
The stars or the cut up pieces?
The sky belongs to no one.
When a bird flies
does its wings lift the whole sky?
When it returns,
are its wings painted the color of the sky?
The shapes
I arrange on paper —
are birds, words, branches, clouds?
If I were a musician
I would have arranged
a bird song in the sky.
If I were a painter,
I would have arranged
spaces and colors in the sky.
The sky is like water.
It never saves footprints.

I struggle to leave footprints.
Footprints on Earth take shape
and then vanish
and again take shape.
I look at the sky and wait
for words to blossom —
buds into flowers.
I wait to find
fragrant tender footprints
in the sky of words.

In the Bazaar

Mother,
how I enjoyed
going to the bazaar with you!
We drove in a horse-buggy with leather seats.
We took a purse, a mesh
of filigreed silken threads,
holding money.

Everyone there knew you.
The shopkeepers
welcomed you warmly.
You bought my favorite
fruit and vegetables
and sometimes even print fabric
my favorite color, rust
for my dress or skirt.

After shopping,
you would order
the same horse-buggy
with the same driver, Fakir,
you had known for years
who brought us home
from every trip to the bazaar.

I remember — once
when you were haggling
with a vegetable vendor
over his prices,
I sneaked away
and got lost
in a toy shop
shutting you out of my mind.

Losing sight of me
you became hysterical,
retracing your steps to the shops
we had visited
asking everyone.
When no one could help you find me,
with tears in your eyes
you stepped into a temple
praying to
Krishna, the Lord Protector
to protect me.
You stopped
at the poor astrologer's sparrow
which, perched in a cage on the city's pavement,
forecasts bright futures for people.
Just when you stood still at last,
not knowing which way to turn,
I emerged from the toy shop.
Our eyes met.
You ran,
took me in your arms,
and hugged me so hard
that I have never been
able to get away
from you.

Mother,
Today, too,
all by myself,
I wander on my bare feet
in a bazaar
among faces that seem familiar
yet remain unknown to me.

4

Empty Forest

Darkness all around.
Empty forest.
Not even a cricket sound.
I am lost in a wooden labyrinth.

I stumble, pass out.
Find myself revived in a strange world
of stretching sand dunes.
Sunrays scream their heat.
Dryness grasps my throat —
can thirst be quenched with wet sand?

I tumble into a canyon
where a rope hangs from above
just beyond my reach.
How do I ascend?

And up above people
watch me, helpless lion in a pit.
They say I'm paying for my sins.

I cannot sleep. This
nightmare shakes the night awake.

Doll House

I live in this home but
I am just a doll
in a doll house
a play thing for many!

Acquaintances arrive
and expect me to converse.
Words freeze when I open my lips.
Tell me, is there an ice
that never melts?

My master
takes me out of the showcase,
makes me sit on the sofa,
caresses me and says —
"Oh, this is a recent illness.
She used to speak volumes,
but now, no such eloquence."
I watch and listen lost.
(What do others know
of the wordless quarrels of couples?)

My chatterbox daughter
tries to feed me
milk from a plastic bottle.
"Oh, you are my real baby," she babbles.
I see myself
in the mirror of her eyes.
I lose control, and pass out silently.
First, I lie flat on the floor
and then vanish under the tightly glued,
hard, square tiles of silence.

Family Portrait

After twenty years
I found my family portrait
Breathing life into
two decades, three generations.

How my father stands out —
a man who embodied
Gandhiji's revolutionary times!
And my mother —
docile, head covered —
a proper Gujarati lady,
despite those modern days of Bombay!
Brothers, with their wives and children
and I among them —
neither here, nor there!

The glaring Sun
squinting everyone's eyes
has entered the photograph
along with chrysanthemums
that will stay fresh
as long as the portrait lives.

In the background
the house with peeling plaster
looks a little old, a little new…

I put away the picture.

The mind flashes
darkness clears for a moment
and I see
things as they are.

On Each October 2, I Have a Dream![1]

"Panna!
Did you ever see Gandhiji?"
A frequent innocent question.
"Yes." I answer.
Then curious eyes, awestruck,
ask: "Where?" "When?" "How?"
I explain:
"When I was very, very young,
father took me every evening
to Gandhiji's prayer meeting on Juhu beach
in Mumbai, close to our bungalow.
We arrived early, so we could sit in the front.
Gandhiji, almost-running, arrives sharply on time.
Mesmerized, I saw him
sitting cross legged, his face radiant
his eyes pools of love.
Then his favorite hymn breaks out,
Vaishnav Jan to Tene Kahiye…"[2]

Following his footsteps, like a million others,
father became a Gandhian.
He went to jail: wore only two sets of homespun clothes;
ate only simple food.
Our Vaishnav family embraced
Gandhiji's insistence on simplicity, truth, and patriotism.

Each October 2, I dream of Gandhiji
In my dream, he asks me —
"You will come to my prayer meeting, won't you?"
And I start singing "Vaishnav Jan to Tene Kahiye…"

Puzzled, my husband asks me in the morning:
Do you know you were singing last night in your sleep?

Hair

Mother combed my hair
when I was a child.

Holding me still in front of her,
sticking a mirror in my hand,
she smeared my hair with
homemade Brahmi oil.
After taking all the tangles out,
parting and braiding my long black hair,
she tied silver bells at the tail end.

She turned me around to face her.
"Did you like the way I combed?"
she asked.
I just smiled.
Sometimes, playfully
she tousled my combed hair;
I'd pretend to be angry.

Today, my hair is short.
Unoiled, it is dry and frazzled:
uncombed, unkempt.

Breathing real anger, I look for my mother.

NOTES FOR PAGE 8

[1] October 2 is Mahatma Gandhiji's birthday

[2] Vaishnav Jan is one of the most popular Hindu Bhajans (devotional lyrics), written in the 15th century by the poet Narsinh Mehta in the Gujarati language. The bhajan was included in Mahatma Gandhiji's daily prayer. The bhajan speaks about the life, ideals, and mentality of a Vaishnav Jan (a follower of Vishnu or Krishna). All the stanzas, basically, list characteristics of an ideal person, especially nonviolence and truthfulness.

And I

Each time after love-making
you drop into slumber,
and I,
keep tossing and turning
in nightmares about my child
never to be born.

I will name him "Vaibhav."
Yes, he will be the "Wealth" of our impoverished lives
that look like a beggar's aluminum bowl,
dented and bent out of shape.

Oh, see, see!
Hear those drumbeats somewhere in the distance!
As the drums beat, fingernails
dig deep into my muscles,
someone is snatching away my "Vaibhav."
I open my weary eyes
and sense a rustle of air
leaving stealthily from under the bed
and sneaking out through the window cracks.

"Vaibhav" has vanished!
Your snoring has subsided.
And I tumble deep down a vale
like a derailed train.

Kanku

"Mommy! Mommy!
Look
her forehead is bleeding!"
An American child's
remark —
innocent enough.
Instinctively
I cover the mark
on my forehead
with my hand.
I see the red smear
of *kanku*
sign of life and good luck
in my open palm
and for a moment
I feel blessed.
I feel again the embrace
of Mother Teresa
the day we met.
But, unlike her, I
can offer neither
blessing nor generosity.
I make a fist
to hide my blood red palm.
My nails dig deep into the skin.
The child was right.
I bleed.

Tulsi[3] Plant

When I light a lamp
I close my eyes and pray
in a temple set in a small corner
of my big house, I remember
my mother praying with her eyes closed.
Walking circles around the Tulsi plant
she sprinkles droplets into the air offering water to the Sun.

Time pushes me back
into the wrinkled tide of childhood —
a small girl
holding onto the edge
of her mother's sari
looking on with curiosity
at the slow process of
mother praying with her eyes closed.

Now I want to know:
Did my mother's prayer for me
get entangled in myriad circles
around the Tulsi plant?

[3] Tulsi is the most sacred herb of India. Tulsi (*Ocimum sanctum*), is also
known as Holy Basil. Tulsi has been revered in India for over five thou-
sand years, as a healing balm for body, mind and spirit, and Hindus
worship it in the morning and evening. It is known to bestow an amazing
number of health benefits.

Broken Button Outside the University Library[4]

A madman wanders
around the white broken button.
He sits down on it and stares into space.
Sometimes, he talks to the steps
which go up and then down,
and return to the button.
He smiles at the closed library windows,
picks up scattered leaves and holds them like a bouquet of
    flowers.
He stares at the faces entering and leaving the library.
Sometimes confused, imploring,
sometimes crying.
He is like a broken button with four holes
and inside,
we are books full of words.

One day he was found
dead on the steps.
We stayed inside
stacking books on the shelves
stacked like books on the shelves.

---

[4] Sculpture outside Van Pelt Library, University of Pennsylvania.

This Ungodly Hour

Between midnight and four a.m.
Brahma's sacred moment —
my mind wakes up
longing to leap out of the body
cuddled in bed, under comforters.

Silence
serrates the sum of yesterdays and todays
and turns into a river flooding my eyes.
I stare at the ceiling through tears;
which dampen the soft cotton pillow
where my head seeks rest.

A breeze feels like a tremor,
as if someone with steel-boots pacing the fresh grass,
suddenly steps on my brittle bones.
I sit up.
Unaware, I fold my hands, bow my head
before Lord Krishna's portrait,
my mother's loving gift,
perched immaculately on the table across the bed.

Mother, you are in heaven
very far from me and yet
you fill this lonely room with memories.
Mother, I wonder whether you can see
or do anything, yet I am tempted to tell you:
many times I have sat here facing Lord Krishna
in this very bed, in this very way
at this ungodly hour
and have felt the sadness of a wet bench
in an isolated garden on a rainy day.

Mother,
the voice you heard in your womb
dissipates in soundless echoes now.
Do you know, mother,
this moment of insight
stands like a crumbling cement wall
between my closed, visionary eyes?

The Witness Candles

A terrace.
An evening.
Rain in the background.
Candles as witnesses.
Two chairs. One couple.
No sooner than they start to talk,
the jealous wind snuffs out
the light of their opening dialogue.
What remains,
is evening
long night,
drenching rain,
and
two still chairs.

Concentration Camp of Amnesia

Go ahead:
Shove me
into the concentration camp of amnesia.
Why do you now
whip me with his name and accusations?
I am tired
of this boring punishment.
I ask for
new violence!

Lioness

You may stroke my neck with fingers now.
I will not roar!
I have become a tamed animal.

No need to worry
I may be dangerous.
See, the pet licks
your hand, your cheek, your nose
and she rolls over at your feet.
Don't you feel the touch of her soft hair?

My needs are few: a little milk and meat;
a small corner in your mansion.
You are a lion and I am
a lioness.

You can lift and throw me in the air.
I won't tear you with my claws.
Here, put your hand on my neck and mouth;
cup my soft muzzle.

See, I am a tamed lioness.

But you don't want me as a pet.
I know, you want to let me loose
somewhere in the Acacia forest.
I also know why. It's because
I refuse to meet your demand.
You want a lioness that never roars.

Oh, naiveté!
No such creature exists.
You seek mythology.

Love's Acreage

A cow starved for grass,
looks restlessly around —
round-eyed, desperate.
Her breathing, in and out,
is all the air
there is.
That's when
a field of grass appears,
just over there,
green, glorious green,
love's acreage —
but in between,
a lake of tears to be crossed.
Herds of cattle
surround
the dream pasture,
a warm circle of kin.
But now her eyes begin
to burn-weighed down,
heavy as hills
however hard she tries to lift them
they remain shut.

Supermarket

Grocery shopping
Saturday's weekly ritual!
My eyes and hands play a familiar game
with prices stamped on shelved items.

Fruit and vegetables
cry out to be freed
from plastic-wrap and air-conditioning.
Lambs hang headless on racks.
I can hear screams of grief
from "boneless chicken, family size."
Milk is "fortified, homogenized,
pasteurized, and vitamins added."
I wonder, how the cows feel!

Words are muffled
amidst people's shuffle.
I only hear the sound
of hustling high heels,
rattle of worn out shopping carts,
and money swallowed by cash registers.

I come out of the supermarket
listening with my eyes,
speaking with my hands.

Elements

My Mother's body:
Earth, Water, Fire, Air, and Space[5]
was turned to ashes
thirty years ago.

And yet, smoke rising
from the pyre burns
my eyes across the ocean.

The warm waters spring up
again and again
lighting the smoke
soothing my burning eyes.

---

[5] The *panchamahabhuta* are the five elements of nature. According to Hindu
mythology, every human body is made essentially from five elements
which are Earth (*bhumi*), Water (*jala*), Fire (*agni*), Air (*vayu*) and Space
(*aakash*). Hindus believe that, upon death; all these five elements of human
body are dissolved to respective element of nature, so that cremation bal-
ances the cycle of nature.

Midnight Questions

While tossing and turning at midnight
questions arose.
Mother,
I am asking questions of you in the morning
the way a friend would ask her close friend.
Mother,
tell me
whether you threw off covers from your mind
during sex?
Was the window shut or open?
Was it a full Moon
or the stars twinkling on a dark night?
Was the intimacy
a climax of your so-called happy married life
or
your decision to "get it over with"?
Did the fragrance of night blooming flowers, all around the house,
touch your bodies?
Were there bells of joy ringing at your lips?
Did your eyes dance?
Did your cheeks glow?
Asking all these questions
knowing your answer is "yes,"
why do I feel that
after sex
a seed of sadness
had been sown in your womb?

Mother

The movements so shapely
in an enduring old lady,
tuneful sounds in her eyes,
and an uninterrupted flow
of lifelong relationship
suddenly silenced.

Your Name on My Palm

I count and recount
slivers of stars on a full-moon night,
opened and half-opened buds of Parijat,
falling white raindrops outside the window.
Suddenly a thought,
like a Kesuda flower,
blossoms.
I take my red pen
and write your name on my palm
and kiss it a hundred times.
For a hundred moments
loneliness disappears
a hundred times.

Fellowship of the Falling Rain

Let me spell out the fellowship
between memories of you and falling rain.

Sometimes,
memories,
are fragrant, invisible.

Sometimes,
evening thunder storms
proclaim the arrival of memories to the world.

And at other times,
torrential rain falls for days.

Ship Lost

Like an exclamation mark
in an unfinished poem,
you suddenly punctuate
the half-way point in my life,
an image of a ship lost
in the Indian Ocean
uncertain of the journey's end.
I can no longer exclaim:
"Why don't you complete the poem?"

Eviction Notice

Just want to inform you that the lease is expiring on your rented house and we do not intend to renew it. Please vacate the house as soon as you receive this letter. It is not your business whether the house will remain empty or is rented to another tenant. Also, you do not have any right to make inquiries regarding this matter. You are forbidden to enter the property in any manner — in thought, in dream, or in any subconscious condition. We will call the police if you try to trespass the property physically or via memory.

Sincerely,

The Landlord

P.S. And yes, we will change the locks after you move out.

Mousetrap

Tempted by a piece of cheese
we adventuresome mice
are caught in mousetraps!
We run the family, do our jobs,
ascend to riches, descend to poverty,
dangling between
necessities and luxuries.

The cheese is already eaten.
The trap-door is open
but no one steps out.
We are outside, we are inside.

Did Someone Say I Left India?

It is long
since I left India.

At the air-conditioned JFK Airport,
dressed in American clothes
I do not draw attention.
Now I do enjoy tea with lemon,
not necessarily with spices.

Also, for some time
the Indian face
in my passport has had
American fingerprints and seals
of official immigration.

Waiting for your arrival,
I pick up the *New York Times*.
While turning the pages
my eyes pause where
the news of India appears.
Reading these items,
my mind returns to girlhood and I visit
my parents' home in Mumbai.
My eyes look for India
in the national and international columns.

I have never left India.

The Protector

Now
with every breath
America enters
and fills my lungs.

The mild fragrance
of her seasonal flowers
becomes a breeze
that moves
through my blood and bones.

Her rains
unaware of seasons
make their home
on the backs of
my fluttering eyelids.

In the wintry snow,
she becomes a shawl
wrapping my neck and shoulders
keeping me warm.

When I visit India
landing at Mumbai Airport
America follows me like a shadow
playing the protector.

Protecting me from whom?
From what?
I cannot tell.

Return

I went home for my Diwali vacation. I saw my mother, father, relatives, and friends. Oh, I also saw my childhood home and the trees still blooming with flowers. My pleasure was a necklace of Marigold flowers. Briefly, I forgot my life and work in America.

Now I am back. No one seems to recognize me: Strange.

My boss is the same. She has the body of a woman and the mind of a man. Highly ambitious, she gives me a masked smile. We get along fine.

Our director is also the same. Fixing his mustache with one hand, and with the other, playing with change in his pants pocket. He goes on expounding on 'duty.'

My colleagues Midori, Wilma, Nancy, Elizabeth, John, Kenny, Bill are all sitting at their desks as always.

Nobody seems to know me now. I feel as if I am new, an unknown here. Sometimes someone smiles and I begin to think maybe…but, oh no! It is but a form.

I slide my swivel chair and face my desk. My books staring at me, my philodendron, and letters saved in the left hand drawer, the computer, and the hanging calendar — they all welcome me with: "Oh, we missed you very much."

Homesickness

Uprooting
a flowering tree
from faraway tropical Mumbai
I replanted it
in Philadelphia's cold, alien soil.
I was absolutely determined
to ensure its survival.
But
when the trees here spew
the sickening pink
of cherry blossoms
I long for
the slow opening
of glowing saffron
Kesuda flowers.
When the hard Earth here splits
and pours forth hot summer roses
my eyes cry red for Gulmohar.
It rains here all year long
But I long for
the lost season of rains,
the monsoon fragrance of India
that still caresses my skin.
Here, we have everything.
And nothing.

I am homesick.
Feel like
packing my bags
and going home…

But where is my home now?

Headlines

A foreigner in the United States sells newspapers
in a stall set up
in the center of Philadelphia.

He sells newspapers for eighteen hours a day.
He sells newspapers in languages known and unknown to him.
He sells newspapers ignoring the noise of the passing trains.
He sells newspapers oblivious of faces coming to his shop.
He sells newspapers to collect dollars.
He sells newspapers to educate his children left behind in his
    country.
He sells newspapers to achieve the American dream.
He sleeps only for an hour or two —
...on the spread-out bed made of unsold newspapers.

Illegal Alien

It has been years since
I deported Memory,
once my constant companion.

Now, just before dawn
I hear whispering.
Is he trying to sneak back in?

Feeling suffocated, I open the window
shut for years.
I hear someone knocking and fling open the door
only to find the wind hissing through the cracks.
I tell myself,
Memory banished
wouldn't return this boldly.

But did he really try to slip in?
I feel disturbed at the thought.
Does he not know
that in America,
an illegal alien is arrested,
handcuffed, jailed, tried in court;
and, if found guilty, deported once more?

When I enter the room I find him
spread over bedsheet folds
disguised as silver moonlight
shining through the open window.

Police tell me:
"Opening the window was your first mistake."

To Live and Rule

I don't believe in
jumping before the train
like Anna Karenina,
swallowing poison
like Madam Bovary,
putting my head in an oven
like Sylvia Plath,
or
breathing carbon monoxide
in a closed garage
like Anne Sexton.
I want to live and rule
like Queen Elizabeth.
I want to be a Renaissance woman.

Women's Freedom

According to men
women's freedom
is a right they bestow upon women
to make this independent decision:
which foot should we plunge
in boiling hot water
and which do we put
on flat tiles of ice!

Blue and Red

Engrossed in the meeting of day and night
I did not realize my foot hit stone.
The wound was much deeper than I felt.
Before I could put my foot under running water
the sky-blue bath tub was stained with twilight colors.
I managed to forget the pain for a while,
put on a bandage that could not dam the blood.
Flowing blood is nothing new to me:
An intimate, steadfast companion!

Arctic Desert

How can I survive
in this Arctic desert without my people?
I try to give birth to them,
dreaming and drawing them out in my sleep.

I sit near the burning window
I see only one thing outside —
a long outstretched space
where the dust of memory rises and falls.
I see the frozen white outside
oblivious of life beneath.
I breathe to feel
my bones, ribs, and intestines.
Are they sound?

Strangers surround me.
(When young, how I avoided going to the bazaar!)
A woman comes and addresses
my plants by children's names.
And a strange man makes advances
to relieve my sadness.
(How can I force a false smile!)
I look for a face which shone
like a Sun,
now lost in the night.

Between your absence
and my existence
a yawn stretches
at the very source of unsung lyrics.

Winter Tears

≈ 1 ≈

Can the Sun's heat
heal
the burns scalded
by winter's ice?

≈ 2 ≈

Between eyelids
spread
tall, wide
heaps
of salt.

Dream Alive

You and I:
separate bodies
of a single soul —
we have run a million miles,
a million strivings
to force this dream alive
but somehow deep somewhere
rings the eternal echo
of split canyons.

We are
two pages in a book
facing each other
bound but separate
sewn together by predestined
mortal ties.

Talk

All our lives
we talked
and talked and talked
about the living room.
I wish
at least once
someday, some night,
we had talked
about the bedroom.

Heart Line

My lifelong desire:
to place my hand in his.
To keep the dream alive
each day I stare at my palm
searching for the heart line
that connects.

At last!
The line arises
and our hands touch!
Claws maul my flesh
and disfigure the skin
of my lifelong desire.

Self Portrait

I wander
Philadelphia streets
with a poet's camera ready to click.
I hope the lenses gather
all the negatives of this world.

Who lives in these houses
lurking behind gated walls?
How many people?
What do they do?

In the evening, are they happy or sad?
At night, do they fly high and glide
in pleasant dreams
or get smashed in a valley of memories?
Are they comforted by their comforters?

I, too, wanted to build a home,
but not of bricks.
I, too, wanted to set up a regime
ruled by love.
I wanted a corner to myself
to pray, not to beg.
I thought the touch of a child's little hands
would turn mine
into fully flowered branches of Gulmohar.
How long can I lie torn
between what could have happened
and what has come to be?

Why do these walls eavesdrop
on my intimacies?
Will they never melt?
How come I succeed in everything

but love?
When love fails,
can life be counted a success?

When I reach ripe old age,
will there be a warm hand left to hold?
Will my words ever
turn into pearls that fit
a true lover's ears?
Or am I damned to stand
before my wardrobe in my old age,
and failing to recognize myself
change the costumes over and over
to play others' roles?

Sometimes I feel that in my own house,
all alone
I should turn off the lights,
and roll around in bed until
creases upon creases upon creases
imprint the sheet!
Then I could tell myself
oh yes!
someone did come and sleep with me,
someone did come and make love to me.
The wrinkled bed is
proof enough!
But oh! I have no other eyewitness
except my pillow to testify
to this make believe.
Can one live an entire life
resting only with a pillow?

What happened to the photos of the world
I wished to click?
My camera has brought home captive
one lone negative!

Curse

I am still searching for
that long-lost ring of recognition
my synonym for happiness.

It must be Durvasa's curse on Shakuntala
visiting me.[6]
Why else would I stare through
the window
waiting for steps
that never appear?

---

[6] In the *Abhijñānashākuntala*, written by Kalidasa, when the maiden Shakuntala
ignored Durvasa's demands to be welcomed as a guest because she was
daydreaming about her lover, Dushyanta, he cursed her that her lover
would forget her. Horrified, Shakuntala's companions managed to mollify
Durvasa, who softened the curse, saying that Dushyanta would remember
Shakuntala when he saw the ring that he gave her as a token of their love.
The sage's curse came true of course and was eventually lifted, just as he
said it would be. By the end of the play, the two lovers are reconciled.

Us

All our lives
we
have seen each other.
I wait at the station
and
you disappear
in a passing train.

Tropical

Let's forget your death and mine
there are other things to remember.

Places where there are no
air-conditioned houses
air-conditioned offices
air-conditioned banks
air-conditioned supermarkets
and air-conditioned cars.

Death is nothing to fear
when the constant company
of this cold, controlled air has made
our body and soul air-conditioned.

We are ready for it when it comes.
So let's forget your death and mine.
Let us open the window facing East
and allow the Sun to ride in
making inner spaces
tropical once again.

Placement

I reorganize my living room
asking each piece
where it would like to be placed.
I give a new spot to the sofa and the lamp,
change the drapes, and
replace the old rug with a wall-to-wall carpet.
The living room with its new decor
looks precise and proper.
When everything is in place
I begin to wonder!
Where should I place myself?

The Spiral Stairs

Entrance to an abandoned house.
The front door opens with the key you already hold.
Your purpose: Find the most important room
without a map or guide.
Climb the spiral stairs.
Bypass corners.
Slowly, doors begin to open.
Windows breathe in the air.
Whatever was foggy becomes clear.
Light spreads everywhere.

Pain
lives in your favorite room.
Continue measuring its walls
foot after foot.
Happiness
steps out of that very room
forgetting all its
measurements and dimensions.

Time in a Suitcase

The morning asks me
what did I do at night?
The night asks me
what did I do all day?
The year-end asks
what did I do all twelve months?
The decades ask me
what did I do all those years?
What did I do? What did I do?
Time needs accountability.
Refusing to answer
I put the time in a suitcase,
lock it,
and shelve it in the attic.
On my return
I am still surrounded by
questions and their foot prints.

Time's Flirtations

Time
makes advances at me.
I rage.
I will have him arrested;
I will seek justice;
I will see him handcuffed, prosecuted, punished,
and sent to jail.
Ashamed of himself
he'll be unable to look me in the eye.

But
time is an escape artist,
no one's been able to nab him.

Sunday

To fill a dull Sunday
I made phone calls
till my finger tired,
but contacting no one
the dial returned to zero.

I watched television
like a camera without film.
Picked up the *New York Times*
a well-stacked newspaper of two hundred pages
very heavy with bloody wars and accidents.

Nothing seemed to change.

Becoming restive
walking out of the house,
I noticed
the evening conversing
with the freshly grown fields of grass
and a bunch of butterflies
assembled to eavesdrop.

I became them
not knowing when.

Japanese Maple

The Japanese maple I planted
has spread out
plunging into my front yard.
Now each summer
this tree with rust leaves rattles
and leans and laughs with the wind.

I wonder whether it remembers Japan.

I remember Mumbai.

Chrysanthemums

Tightly arranged chrysanthemums
in a painted glass vase
wilted now in stale water.

Suddenly
a hand's blow
smashes their small world.
Water splashes on the floor.
And the harmonized petals scatter.
Fusion tumbles into disorder.

How do I recreate a flower
from disintegrated petals?

Sunflower

Despite the quickening dusk,
a sudden hush of the wind,
and a hasty flight of birds bound home,
why do I feel
like an open sunflower?

Jasmines

Jasmines
plucked in a dream
are long lost;
but why does their fragrance
still stick to my fingers?

Tapestry of Stars

Sitting on a lake's bank
I immerse my hand
in its calm waters
gathering
the tapestry of stars.
The water's fabric shakes and
creases.
The stars scatter
and moisten my hand.

Ripple

The wind's hand
shook
while writing a poem
on water.

Memory

A doe
steps outside its park
and suddenly dances
on lush green grass.
It plays with Sun's splendor
jumping around rolling and rolling.

Installation

We take their pulse every day;
careful their blood flow is clear
their green laughter, fresh
their posture, erect.

We watch
their taste and diet.
We install them in macramé pots,
feed them Miracle-Gro
quench their thirst.

Could it be that house plants
are the conscious beings
and we, merely their attendants
sterile plastic slaves?

Obstruction

There was nothing in this large room
but just us!
Now it is filled:
a Scandinavian sofa set, a coffee table,
lamps with Kashmir carvings,
a tapestry of a king's procession running across the wall;
and then, yes, the plants
springtime everywhere
in this dull square space.

How these objects obstruct
my coming to you!

Acrobat of Love

Lying in bed
staring at the ceiling
I felt like reaching out,
it seemed so close.

My fingers failing to touch it,
I place chair upon chair upon chair
on my bed,
standing atop
this pyramid
like an acrobat of love
still unable
to touch the surface
that seemed so close.

I cannot figure out
whether
the ceiling is too far
or
my arms too short.

Green-Grape Tear

Hand in hand and empty-handed.
Lip on lip but disconnected.
The final embrace.
Footsteps then in opposite directions
two branches of one tree cut.
Twilight:
the pond
a translucent silver-green
grape of a tear
containing, reflecting
everything.

Rains Moist as Fire

Is it possible
when you are with me
I find
butterflies more vibrant,
each blade of grass a green lamp,
and the rains moist as fire?

Small Terraces

This body
is a skyscraper.
No place
to build an awning.
And that's why
I have treasured you
behind my eyes, small terraces.
They do not close.
Used to sweet water lakes,
you may singe in this hot reservoir!

Indecision

A silver fish
wavers between
the dark ocean depths
and its shimmering surface
then, lands silent on the shore!

Curiosity

Going round and round the Moon
upon lake's calm waters
a silver fish looks up and wonders
why doesn't the Moon swim?

Desert Swimming

How does one understand
this desperate struggle for survival?
You suggest I ask a fish
tossed out of water.

But how do you define
the fate of living right beneath
the roaring ocean and yet
doomed to swim in a desert?

The Winged World

No movement.
Wind holds its breath.
A muted ambiance where
I can hear
grass sieving the air.
A bee surfaces from the winged world
clattering.
It visits a grass blade for a while
(disinterested)
and flies away.

The crimped grass blade
straightens and inhales.

The Naïve One

Dissatisfied
with the Earth
the butterfly flits off
winging to the sky
higher — still higher than those blossoming
branches near the cloud.
Oh, but the naïve one
does not know —
there is no flower in the cloud.

Almost Born

≈ 1 ≈

A swallowtail
intoxicates the air
hovering
over an island of azaleas;
then flies off,
as if
a poem—almost born—
has vanished.

≈ 2 ≈

When you arrive,
the scattered
drifting words
of my unfinished notes
become a harmony.

Teen Patti

Teen Patti[7] card sessions
every Saturday night,
thousands of rupees change hands;
eyes feast on Asian delicacies,
Indian laughter
drowns Ravi Shankar's sitar.

We talk
of husbands and children;
of ornaments, saris, servants;
of recipes, parties,
and, of course, of other women.
But how come your eyes
remain uncircled by blue boredom?
How well-adjusted you must be!

I, too, find safety
in your gossiping group sometimes,
but now and then,
as I sit in the same room,
your voice becomes an echo
heard over remote Teen Patti sounds
whispering of other places,
other times,
and other worlds.

---

[7] Teen Patti means "three cards." It is an Indian card game, also known as
Flush.

Customs Officer

At Philadelphia airport
the customs officer
suspected me of hiding taxable items.
My facial expression gave me away.
How could I explain
everything I had to declare?
He made me open
the twenty-nine inch bag.
Rifled through all the items
and finally at the very bottom
found an envelope stuffed
with dry flower petals
grown in my Mumbai garden,
a contraband here.

Iceberg

Voyaging through my dead poem.
you won't find anything.
You'd better bury it.
Unless,
digging to the poem's core,
you find
the desolation of wrecked ships
and among them
standing, solid for years,
a towering iceburg,
unbroken.

Open Window

I stand at the open window. No, I won't budge an inch.
Let the pouring rain drench me.
The monsoons of home
never cast such a spell till today.
For ages
I stayed dry,
dry
as these dry-cleaned
drapes,
window always closed
against the rain.
Today, the window
all the way open,
leaves me heavy with wetness.
Let the rain come down
like my hair when the pins
are drawn.
Let it come down.
Let it drown me.
Let it soak the drapes
the carpet, the furniture.
Let the wind howl like a feral cat
wild in the lifeless living room.
Let the dead wood of this house
sing the song of water.

And with it, a simple happiness,
mine, singing the rain's song.

Clouds

These dark rain clouds at noon —
yet my eyes see only
the concealed sky blue
the color of your heart's horizons.

You came knocking at evening
but I heard nothing for a long time.
When I finally opened the door
and smelled the trees
from your body, rain-wet,
only then did I recall
the clouds at noon:
their promise.

Monsoon

The Aashadh monsoon
may arrive on time or not
piercing the dark face of clouds
but this lake of tears
keeps overflowing.
What if it should dry up!
Won't these two little fish,
thirsty for years,
waste away?

Cloud Touches

The ocean breath
in a cloud
touches
the far away sky.
You are
much closer.

Trail

In the evening's half light,
obstructing my dreams,
stand
those trees
naked,
sterile deserts and broken pieces of sky…

To get past them
to get through
the narrow winding trail of life!

Union

Every morning
when I light a lamp
in homage to Lord Krishna's icon
a blazing cremation pyre
stings my eyes.
Both lamp and pyre are fire in shape and color.
Both are holy offerings to God.

An unusual brightness lights up my face.
I know it's a reflection of His radiance.
The atmosphere resonates
the music proclaiming the Union.
My garments fall off.
I become the flame.
I become one with fire
and my spirit abandons the body.

Krishna's outstretched hands clasp me
What remains on Earth
are only my ashes.

To the Beloved Who Came to See the Dead Lover

How can I complain now
about your arriving late?
people are present here and
my lips sealed.

My Poetry. My Planet.

It bears my strength
Betrays my weakness
My face without any make-up
The core of my thought
Truth captured in my eyes
Transparency of glass
Lava of my emotions
The voice for repressed women's suppressed feelings
A nudge to snug society
The planet's blueness
The fragrance of the world's flowers
The landscape of butterflies
Greatness of friendship
Fulfillment of Love
No bitterness
No yesterdays
No tomorrows
No desire to leave any imprint
Just seizing the moment.

Footprints

Resting my index finger on my cheek
I sit in my chair
staring
at vanishing wet footprints
on the sun-swept floor.

HAIKU

1

At dawn
leaves whisper —
the wind's prayer

» ◇ «

2

Constant search
if only I could find a brush
to paint my dreams

» ◇ «

3

Dark stage
Snowflakes dance to
the wind's drumbeat

» ◇ «

4

Dew
etches designs
on a rose petal

» ◇ «

5

Don't know why
no sooner I put on boots
tender grass quivers

» ◇ «

6

Drenched
in this torrential
memory deluge

» ◇ «

7

Every evening
sunlight slides
on hill slopes

» ◊ «

8

Film of dreams
washed away
at first eye blink

» ◊ «

9

Infant sunlight
crawls
near the bed

» ◊ «

10

It wasn't the stone:
the grass carpet
betrayed my feet

» ◇ «

11

Late evening –
the wind searches for keys
in slumbering grass

» ◇ «

12

Memory —
a nimble doe
untrapable

» ◇ «

13

No matter
how much dust blows
flowers are never coated

» ◇ «

14

On the grass
the sunshine jumps —
a yellow rabbit

» ◇ «

15

Silent snow
Four footprints
conversing

» ◇ «

16

Steady, be steady!
The wind's plea
to the candle flame

》 ◇ 《

17

Streaks of light —
shimmering fish
on still waters

》 ◇ 《

18

Sunlight
wipes away wet footprints
from the floor

》 ◇ 《

19

Sunshine on the wall
the wind as its brush
many paintings

» ◇ «

20

The fan turns
calendar leaves —
the wall, mute

» ◇ «

21

The fish wanders
looking for home
in mid-ocean

» ◇ «

22

The Earth, radiant
wears a veil of
tender grass blades

» ◇ «

23

The hills, flooded
in a downpour of
torrential fog

» ◇ «

24

The train leaves —
this handkerchief, wet
is unable to wave

» ◇ «

25

Vast ocean
salted with
the tears of fish

» ◇ «

26

Winter sunlight
shivers, hunts for
a quilt throughout the house

» ◇ «

27

You get up —
these timid bangles
quiver

» ◇ «

28

Your memory —
the touch
of a silk sari softness

» ◇ «

ABOUT THE AUTHOR

A distinguished Indian poet, Panna Naik has been active on the Gujarati literary front for about four decades and has established herself as a major writer. She has written ten volumes of path breaking poetry and a volume of short stories. She has given a distinct voice to the women of India as evidenced by her worldwide following among Indian women. Her poetry has been amply recognized and awarded by the Gujarati literary establishment both in India and in the United States. In addition,  she has done pioneering work in the teaching of Gujarati language as Adjunct Professor at the University of Pennsylvania.

PRAISE FOR *THE ASTROLOGER'S SPARROW*

Reflections on Panna Naik's
The Astrologer's Sparrow ...

Like Yeats's fantasy birds that would sing "of what is past, or passing, or to come," Panna Naik's *The Astrologer's Sparrow* sings of the puzzles of life and riddles of existence. Every poem here is an encounter with a truth one was too lethargic to note or too timid to sound, but which now dawns with the radical suddenness of a revelation.

Her images, tender or etched with the sharpness of steel, ignite a reflection that liberates the mind and illuminates the life lived and forgotten. To read her poems is really to experience the heaving ocean that, for a receptive mind, storms behind ordinary objects of the world. An encounter with this book is a commencement of self-renewal.

Panna's remorseless detachment recalls the objectivity of Wallace Stevens, even as her daring imagination resonates with echoes of Emily Dickinson. As her poem "Iceberg" says, "digging to the poem's core/ you find/ the desolation of wrecked ships." Maybe so, but one thing is certain: Panna Naik's ship, laden with fresh and dazzling poetic tropes, has truly arrived.

This slim volume of poems will delight the novice and challenge the old lovers of poetry.

—**Pradyumna S. Chauhan**
Professor of English
Arcadia University

CPSIA information can be obtained
at www.ICGtesting.com
Printed in the USA
JSHW021939170722
28205JS00002B/75

9 781732 698819